COMPOSER SHOWCASE
HAL LEONARD
STUDENT PIANO LIBRARY

Whispering Woods

NINE PIANO SOLOS WITH OPTIONAL TEACHER DUETS

BY LYNDA LYBECK-ROBINSON

ISBN 978-1-5400-2661-3

Visit Hal Leonard Online at
www.halleonard.com

Contact Us:
Hal Leonard
7777 West Bluemound Road
Milwaukee, WI 53213
Email: info@halleonard.com

In Europe contact:
Hal Leonard Europe Limited
Distribution Centre, Newmarket Road
Bury St Edmunds, Suffolk, IP33 3YB
Email: info@halleonardeurope.com

In Australia contact:
Hal Leonard Australia Pty. Ltd.
4 Lentara Court
Cheltenham, Victoria, 3192 Australia
Email: info@halleonard.com.au

CONTENTS

Performance Notes

Cabin Dance

This high-energy, syncopated piece reflects the spicy, buoyant energy of a South American folk dance. The melody imitates a pair of dancers by moving back and forth between the hands, and the work is punctuated by a dramatic chord punch at the end of each section. Written in C position, this piece is remarkable for sounding more difficult than it is.

Cool, Shade!

Written in the D Dorian mode, this jazzy piece introduces the 5/4 time signature. With a repeating theme and a steady optional accompaniment, the piece gives the impression of difficulty while the performer plays with an easy groove.

Feels Like Spring

Starting in the C position, this piece moves positions in the B section to add another lift to this catchy melody. Like two dancers in step to a foxtrot, this moves around the keyboard more than the other pieces and features lively interaction between the hands.

Gold Creek

"Gold Creek" inspires the atmosphere of an "old-timey" knee-slapping church revival during the 1880s California gold rush. Added to the mix is an echo of the blues, a pinch of jazz, and bright, bold chords—bringing lively fun to the performer and listener!

Little Bear Tango

Inspired by Argentinean composer Astor Piazzola's *Libertango*, this dashing piece in D position is relatively easy to play and wildly infectious! With a left-hand crossover on two occasions, and a bold open-5th interval exchanged between hands in the B section, the pianist enjoys the drama of the tango dance!

Loon Song

The cry of the loon is occasionally mistaken for the distant call of a wolf or the moon howl of a coyote. Reminiscent of the loon's naturally melancholic intervals, a tender melody emerges here, unfolding slowly in this expressive work. Written in middle C position, the right hand frequently crosses finger 2 over 1 providing a new but simple technical challenge.

Moongaze

The bright sounding Lydian mode suggests a sense of wonder in this new age piece. The right hand carries most of the melody while the left hand provides a gentle support with intervals of 2nds, 3rds, and 4ths. The frequent left-hand crossovers add even more dimension to the shimmering melody.

Whispering Woods

This mystical waltz in A minor inspires thoughts of the mysterious and wondrous sounds of a Pacific Northwest rain forest at night. It can be described as slightly eerie with a rich melody and unusual harmonic twists. Left-hand fingering includes 2-over-1 crossing, and the diminished intervals in the B section contribute an intriguing color to this dance.

The Wishing Trees

The gently swaying "Wishing Trees" features a hard-to-forget, romantic melody that glides between the hands. Written in the key of C, the accidentals lean delicately up or down with fingering 2 crossing over 1, adding to the ambience of softly swaying branches in a breeze. The accompaniment complements the piece beautifully, entering at measure 8, following the solo's wistful beginning.

–Lynda Lybeck-Robinson

for Ellizel Simbajon Usi

Cabin Dance

By Lynda Lybeck-Robinson

Accompaniment (Student plays one octave higher than written.)

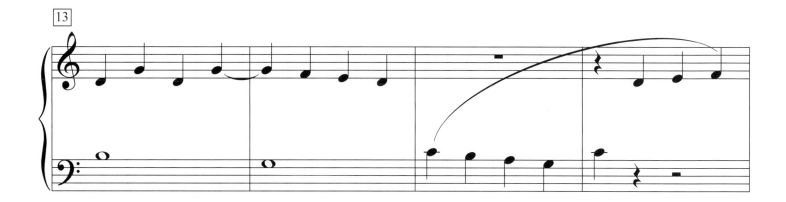

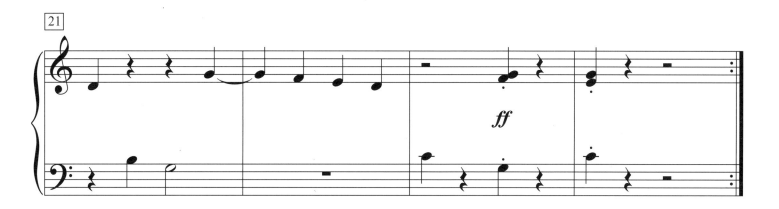

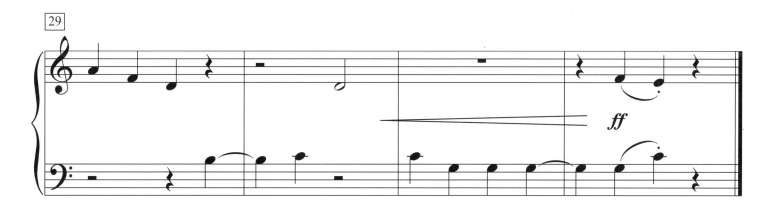

for Cheryl Shockey and Marilyn Dresser

Cool, Shade!

By Lynda Lybeck-Robinson

Accompaniment (Student plays one octave higher than written.)

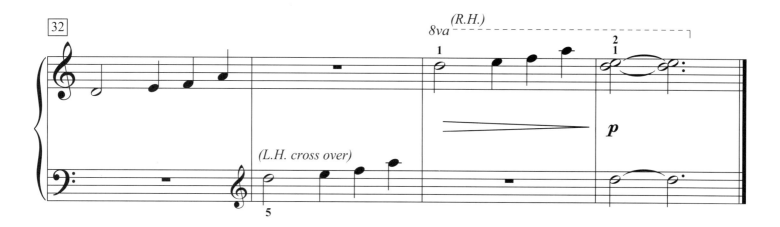

for Amy Rose and Arne Knudsen

Feels Like Spring

By Lynda Lybeck-Robinson

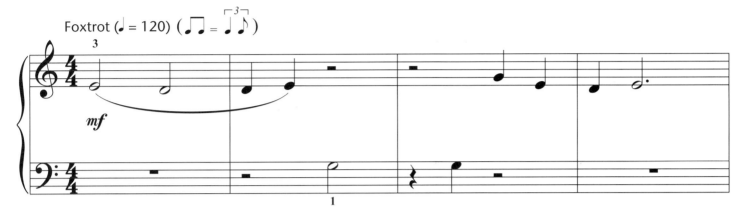

Accompaniment (Student plays one octave higher than written.)

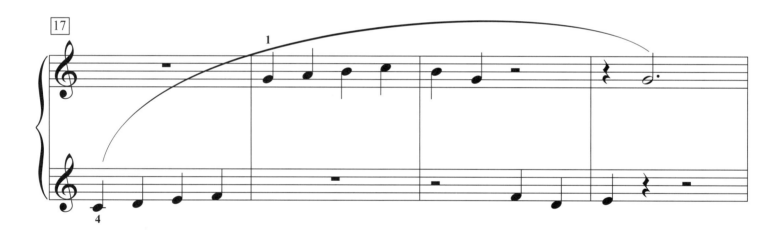

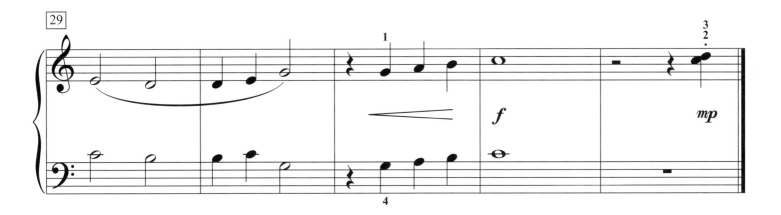

for Morgann Monet Machálek

Gold Creek

By Lynda Lybeck-Robinson

Upbeat Gospel feel (♩ = 168)

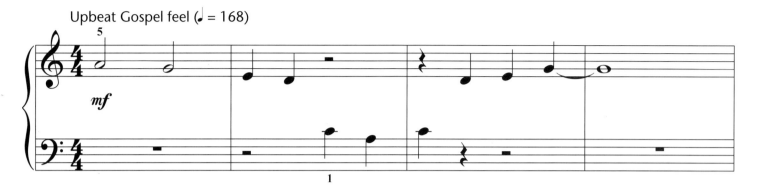

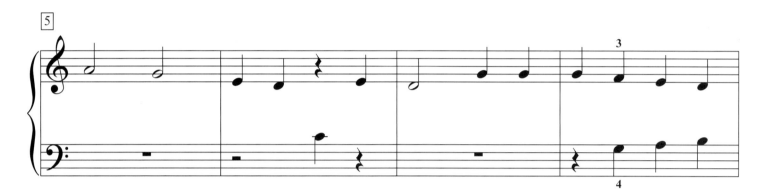

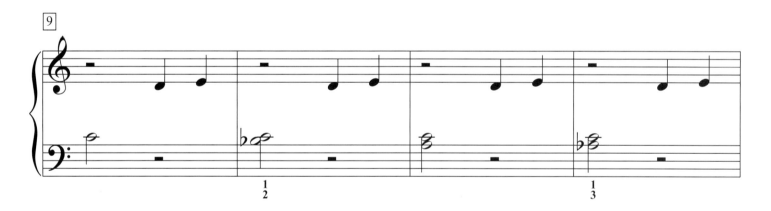

Accompaniment (Student plays one octave higher than written.)

Upbeat Gospel feel (♩ = 168)

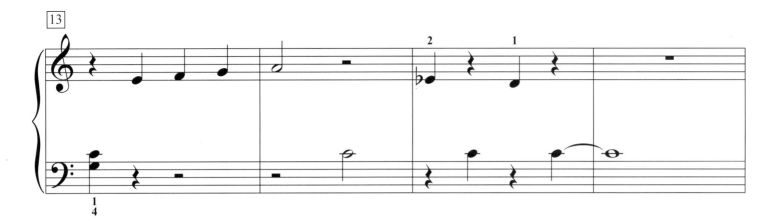

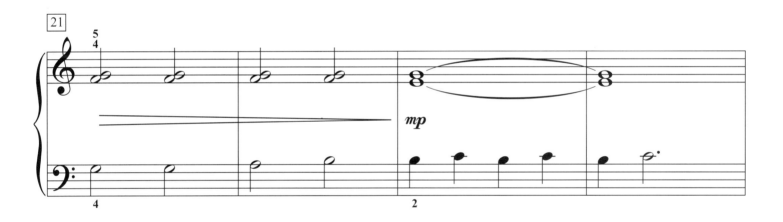

15

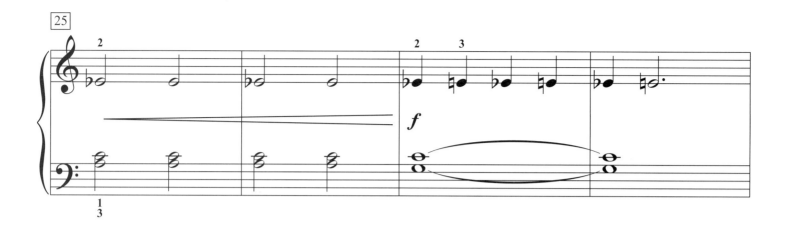

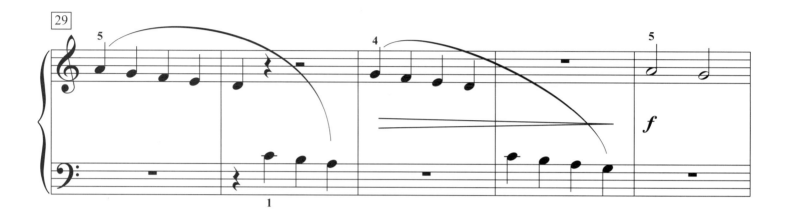

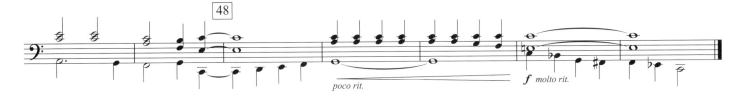

for Ann Kakugawa Fernandez

Little Bear Tango

By Lynda Lybeck-Robinson

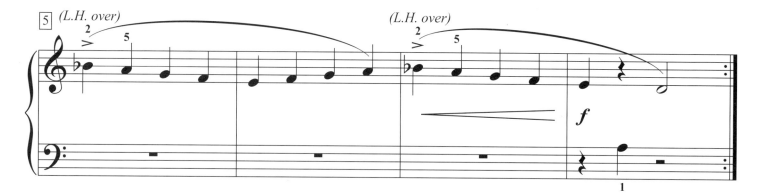

Accompaniment (Student plays one octave higher than written.)

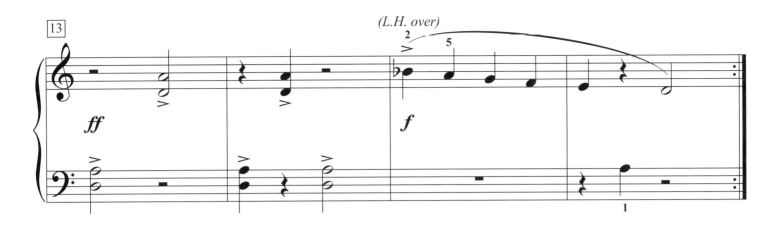

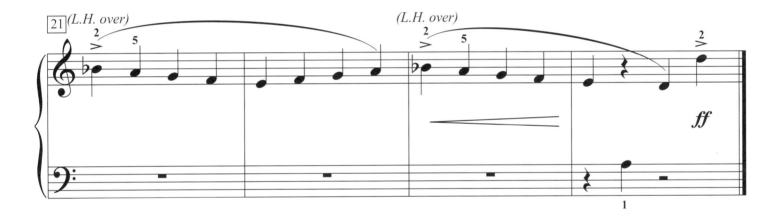

for Kim Groves Brand

Loon Song

By Lynda Lybeck-Robinson

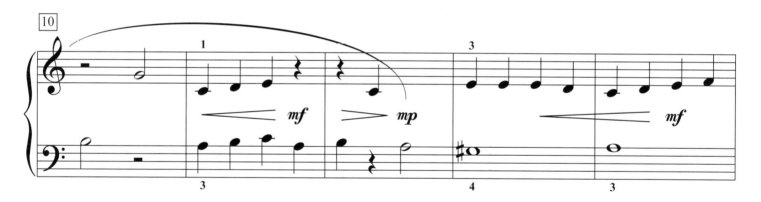

Accompaniment (Student plays one octave higher than written.)

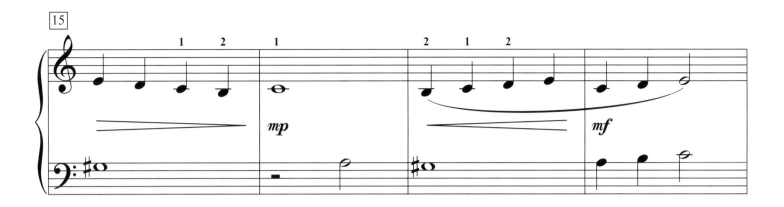

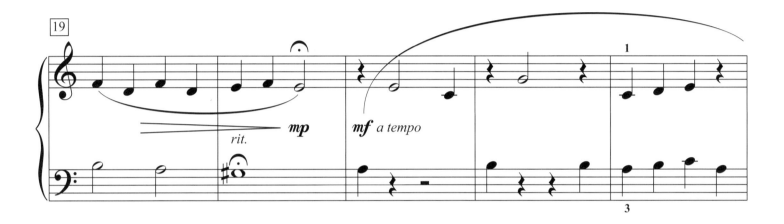

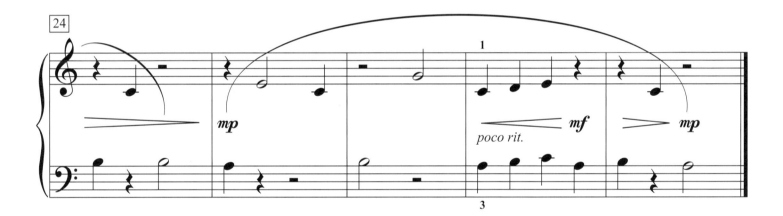

for Lily Marie Mahoney

Moongaze

By Lynda Lybeck-Robinson

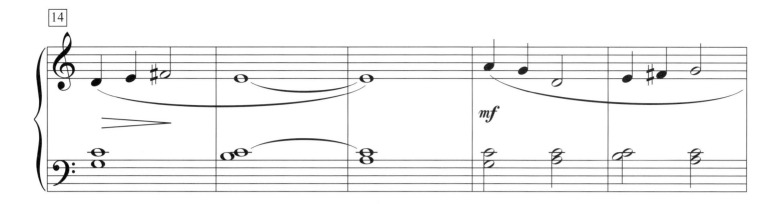

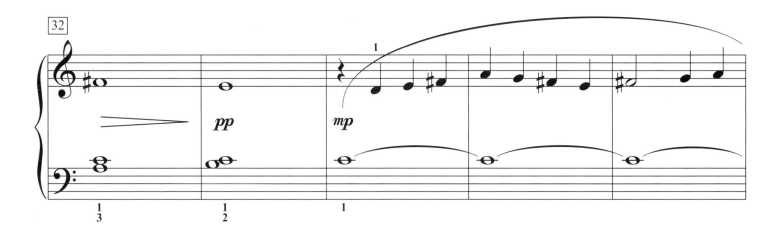

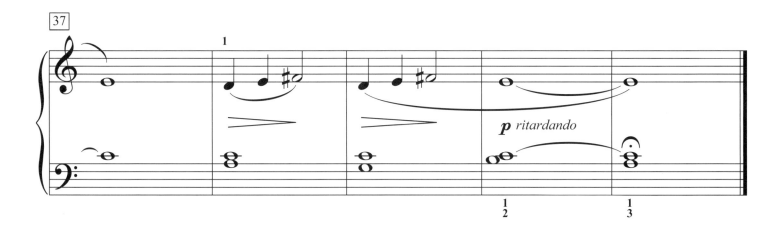

for Natahlie Leksmi O Namasivayam

Whispering Woods

By Lynda Lybeck-Robinson

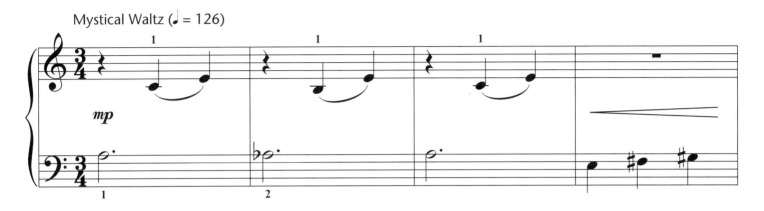

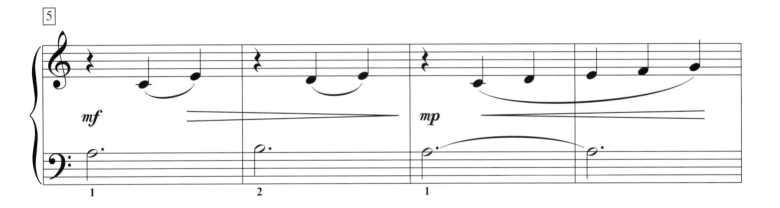

Accompaniment (Student plays one octave higher than written.)

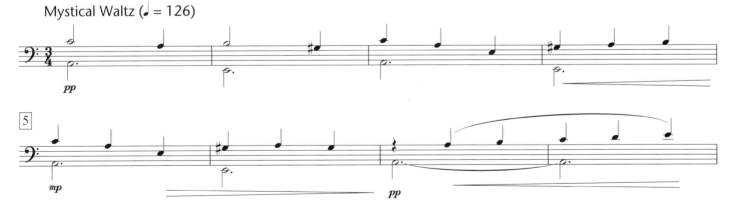

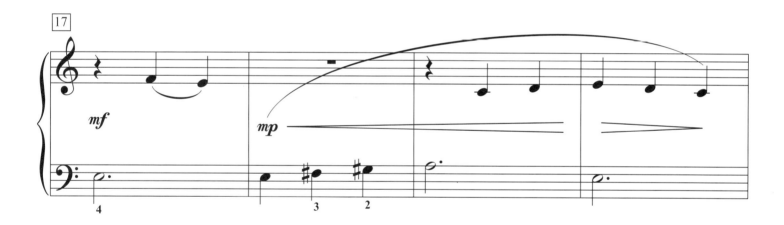

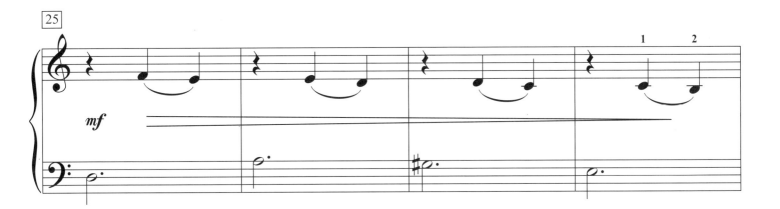

(L.H. over)

for Xavia Jolie Valverde

The Wishing Trees

By Lynda Lybeck-Robinson

Gently swaying (♩ = 126)

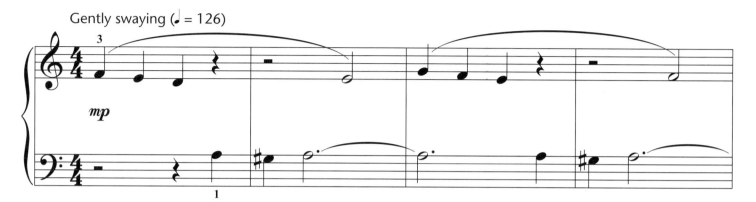

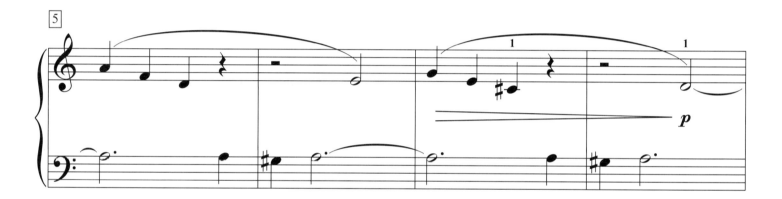

Accompaniment (Student plays one octave higher than written.)

Gently swaying (♩ = 126)

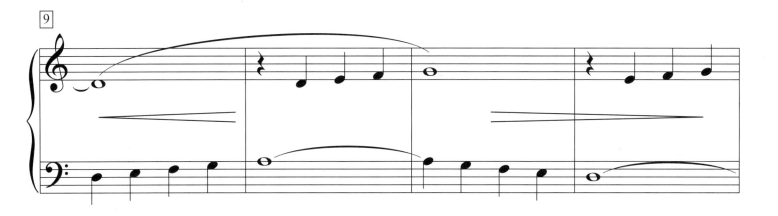

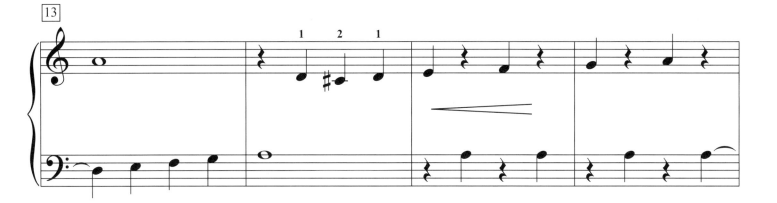

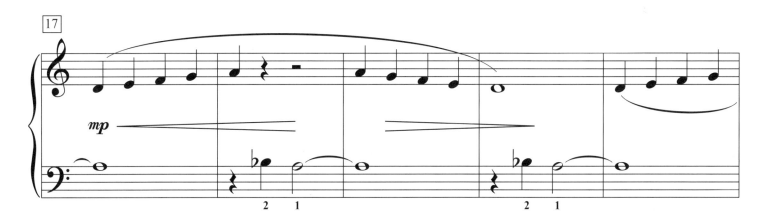

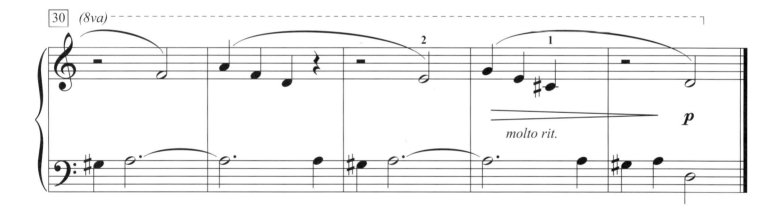

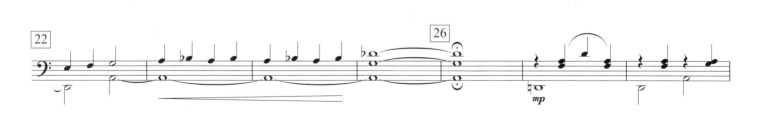

COMPOSER SHOWCASE
HAL LEONARD STUDENT PIANO LIBRARY

This series showcases great original piano music from our **Hal Leonard Student Piano Library** family of composers. Carefully graded for easy selection.

BILL BOYD

JAZZ BITS (AND PIECES)
Early Intermediate Level
00290312 11 Solos..$7.99

JAZZ DELIGHTS
Intermediate Level
00240435 11 Solos..$7.99

JAZZ FEST
Intermediate Level
00240436 10 Solos..$8.99

JAZZ PRELIMS
Early Elementary Level
00290032 12 Solos..$7.99

JAZZ SKETCHES
Intermediate Level
00220001 8 Solos..$8.99

JAZZ STARTERS
Elementary Level
00290425 10 Solos..$7.99

JAZZ STARTERS II
Late Elementary Level
00290434 11 Solos..$7.99

JAZZ STARTERS III
Late Elementary Level
00290465 12 Solos..$8.99

THINK JAZZ!
Early Intermediate Level
00290417 Method Book..................................$12.99

TONY CARAMIA

JAZZ MOODS
Intermediate Level
00296728 8 Solos..$6.95

SUITE DREAMS
Intermediate Level
00296775 4 Solos..$6.99

SONDRA CLARK

THREE ODD METERS
Intermediate Level
00296472 3 Duets..$6.95

MATTHEW EDWARDS

CONCERTO FOR YOUNG PIANISTS
FOR 2 PIANOS, FOUR HANDS
Intermediate Level Book/CD
00296356 3 Movements $19.99

CONCERTO NO. 2 IN G MAJOR
FOR 2 PIANOS, 4 HANDS
Intermediate Level Book/CD
00296670 3 Movements..............................$17.99

PHILLIP KEVEREN

MOUSE ON A MIRROR
Late Elementary Level
00296361 5 Solos..$7.99

MUSICAL MOODS
Elementary/Late Elementary Level
00296714 7 Solos..$5.95

SHIFTY-EYED BLUES
Late Elementary Level
00296374 5 Solos..$7.99

CAROL KLOSE

THE BEST OF CAROL KLOSE
Early Intermediate to Late Intermediate Level
00146151 15 Solos..$12.99

CORAL REEF SUITE
Late Elementary Level
00296354 7 Solos..$6.99

DESERT SUITE
Intermediate Level
00296667 6 Solos..$7.99

FANCIFUL WALTZES
Early Intermediate Level
00296473 5 Solos..$7.95

GARDEN TREASURES
Late Intermediate Level
00296787 5 Solos..$7.99

ROMANTIC EXPRESSIONS
Intermediate/Late Intermediate Level
00296923 5 Solos..$8.99

WATERCOLOR MINIATURES
Early Intermediate Level
00296848 7 Solos..$7.99

JENNIFER LINN

AMERICAN IMPRESSIONS
Intermediate Level
00296471 6 Solos..$8.99

ANIMALS HAVE FEELINGS TOO
Early Elementary/Elementary Level
00147789 8 Solos..$7.99

CHRISTMAS IMPRESSIONS
Intermediate Level
00296706 8 Solos..$8.99

JUST PINK
Elementary Level
00296722 9 Solos..$8.99

LES PETITES IMAGES
Late Elementary Level
00296664 7 Solos..$8.99

LES PETITES IMPRESSIONS
Intermediate Level
00296355 6 Solos..$7.99

REFLECTIONS
Late Intermediate Level
00296843 5 Solos..$7.99

TALES OF MYSTERY
Intermediate Level
00296769 6 Solos..$8.99

LYNDA LYBECK-ROBINSON

ALASKA SKETCHES
Early Intermediate Level
00119637 8 Solos..$7.99

AN AWESOME ADVENTURE
Late Elementary Level
00137563 ....$7.99

FOR THE BIRDS
Early Intermediate/Intermediate Level
00237078 ....$8.99

WHISPERING WOODS
Late Elementary Level
00275905 9 Solos..$8.99

MONA REJINO

CIRCUS SUITE
Late Elementary Level
00296665 5 Solos..$6.99

COLOR WHEEL
Early Intermediate Level
00201951 6 Solos..$8.99

JUST FOR KIDS
Elementary Level
00296840 8 Solos..$7.99

MERRY CHRISTMAS MEDLEYS
Intermediate Level
00296799 5 Solos..$8.99

MINIATURES IN STYLE
Intermediate Level
00148088 6 Solos..$8.99

PORTRAITS IN STYLE
Early Intermediate Level
00296507 6 Solos..$8.99

EUGÉNIE ROCHEROLLE

CELEBRATION SUITE
Intermediate Level
00152724 3 Duets (1 Piano, 4 Hands)...............$8.99

**ENCANTOS ESPAÑOLES
(SPANISH DELIGHTS)**
Intermediate Level
00125451 6 Solos..$8.99

JAMBALAYA
Intermediate Level
00296654 Ensemble (2 Pianos, 8 Hands).........$10.99

JAMBALAYA
Intermediate Level
00296725 Piano Duo (2 Pianos)......................$7.95

LITTLE BLUES CONCERTO
FOR 2 PIANOS, 4 HANDS
Early Intermediate Level
00142801 Piano Duo (2 Pianos, 4 Hands)........$12.99

TOUR FOR TWO
Late Elementary Level
00296832 6 Duets..$7.99

TREASURES
Late Elementary/Early Intermediate Level
00296924 7 Solos..$8.99

JEREMY SISKIND

BIG APPLE JAZZ
Intermediate Level
00278209 8 Solos..$8.99

MYTHS AND MONSTERS
Late Elementary/Early Intermediate Level
00148148 9 Solos..$7.99

CHRISTOS TSITSAROS

DANCES FROM AROUND THE WORLD
Early Intermediate Level
00296688 7 Solos..$6.95

LYRIC BALLADS
Intermediate/Late Intermediate Level
00102404 6 Solos..$8.99

POETIC MOMENTS
Intermediate Level
00296403 8 Solos..$8.99

SEA DIARY
Early Intermediate Level
00253486 9 Solos..$8.99

SONATINA HUMORESQUE
Late Intermediate Level
00296772 3 Movements $6.99

SONGS WITHOUT WORDS
Intermediate Level
00296506 9 Solos..$9.99

THREE PRELUDES
Early Advanced Level
00130747 ....$8.99

THROUGHOUT THE YEAR
Late Elementary Level
00296723 12 Duets..$6.95

ADDITIONAL COLLECTIONS

AMERICAN PORTRAITS
by Wendy Stevens
Intermediate Level
00296817 6 Solos..$7.99

AT THE LAKE
by Elvina Pearce
Elementary/Late Elementary Level
00131642 10 Solos and Duets..........................$7.99

COUNTY RAGTIME FESTIVAL
by Fred Kern
Intermediate Level
00296882 7 Rags..$7.99

LITTLE JAZZERS
by Jennifer Watts
Elementary/Late Elementary Level
00154573 Solos..8.99

PLAY THE BLUES!
by Luann Carman (Method Book)
Early Intermediate Level
00296357 10 Solos..$9.99

Prices, contents, and availability subject
to change without notice.

0518

HAL•LEONARD®
www.halleonard.com

Piano Recital Showcase

"What should my students play for the recital?" This series provides easy answers to this common question. For these winning collections, we've carefully selected some of the most popular and effective pieces from the **Hal Leonard Student Library** – from early-elementary to late-intermediate levels. You'll love the variety of musical styles found in each book.

PIANO RECITAL SHOWCASE PRE-STAFF
Pre-Staff Early Elementary Level
8 solos: Bumper Cars • Cherokee Lullaby • Fire Dance • The Hungry Spider • On a Magic Carpet • One, Two, Three • Pickled Pepper Polka • Pumpkin Song.
00296784 ....$7.99

BOOK 1
Elementary Level
12 solos: B.B.'s Boogie • In My Dreams • Japanese Garden • Jazz Jig • Joyful Bells • Lost Treasure • Monster March • Ocean Breezes • Party Cat Parade • Rainy Day Play • Sledding Fun • Veggie Song.
00296749 ....$8.99

BOOK 2
Late-Elementary Level
12 solos: Angelfish Arabesque • The Brontosaurus Bop • From the Land of Make-Believe • Ghosts of a Sunken Pirate Ship • The Happy Walrus • Harvest Dance • Hummingbird (L'oiseau-mouche) • Little Bird • Quick Spin in a Fast Car • Shifty-Eyed Blues • The Snake Charmer • Soft Shoe Shuffle.
00296748 ....$8.99

BOOK 3
Intermediate Level
10 solos: Castilian Dreamer • Dreaming Song • Jump Around Rag • Little Mazurka • Meaghan's Melody • Mountain Splendor • Seaside Stride • Snap to It! • Too Cool to Fool • Wizard's Wish.
00296747 ....$8.99

BOOK 4
Late-Intermediate Level
8 solos: Berceuse for Janey • Cafe Waltz • Forever in My Heart • Indigo Bay • Salsa Picante • Sassy Samba • Skater's Dream • Twilight on the Lake.
00296746 ....$8.99

CHRISTMAS EVE SOLOS
Intermediate Level
Composed for the intermediate level student, these pieces provide fresh and substantial repertoire for students not quite ready for advanced piano literature. Includes: Auld Lang Syne • Bring a Torch, Jeannette, Isabella • Coventry Carol • O Little Town of Bethlehem • Silent Night • We Wish You a Merry Christmas • and more.
00296877...$8.99

DUET FAVORITES
Intermediate Level
Five original duets for one piano, four hands from top composers Phillip Keveren, Eugénie Rocherolle, Sondra Clark and Wendy Stevens. Includes: Angel Falls • Crescent City Connection • Prime Time • A Wind of Promise • Yearning.
00296898..$9.99

FESTIVAL FAVORITES, BOOK 1
10 OUTSTANDING NFMC SELECTED SOLOS
Late Elementary/Early Intermediate Level
Proven piano solos fill this compilation of selected gems chosen for various National Federation of Music Clubs (NFMC) Junior Festival lists. Titles: Candlelight Prelude • Crazy Man's Blues • I've Gotta Toccata • Pagoda Bells • Tarantella • Toccata Festivo • Tonnerre sur les plaines (Thunder on the Plains) • Twister • Way Cool! • Wild Robot.
00118198..$10.99

FESTIVAL FAVORITES, BOOK 2
10 OUTSTANDING NFMC SELECTED SOLOS
Intermediate/Late Intermediate Level
Book 2 features: Barcarolle Impromptu • Cathedral Echoes (Harp Song) • Dance of the Trolls • Jasmine in the Mist • Jesters • Maestro, There's a Fly in My Waltz • Mother Earth, Sister Moon • Northwoods Toccata • Sounds of the Rain • Un phare dans le brouillard (A Lighthouse in the Fog).
00118202..$10.99

FESTIVAL GEMS – BOOK 1
Elementary/Late Elementary Level
This convenient collection features 10 NFMC-selected piano solos: Brooklyn's Waltz • Chimichanga Cha-Cha • Feelin' Happy • Footprints in the Snow • Lazy Daisy • New Orleans Jamboree • PBJ Blues • Pepperoni Pizza • Sneakin' Cake • Things That Go Bump in the Night. (Note: Solos are from previous NFMC lists.)
00193548 ....$10.99

HAL•LEONARD®

Visit our website at
www.halleonard.com/hlspl
for all the newest titles in this series
and other books in the Hal Leonard
Student Piano Library.

FESTIVAL GEMS – BOOK 2
Early Intermediate/Intermediate Level
Book 2 includes: Caravan • Chatterbox • In the Groove • Jubilation! • Kokopelli (Invention in Phrygian Mode) • La marée de soir (Evening Tide) • Reverie • Time Travel • Voiliers dans le vent (Sailboats in the Wind) • Williwaw.
00193587 ....$10.99

FESTIVAL GEMS – BOOK 3
Late Intermediate/Early Advanced Level
8 more NFMC-selected piano solos, including: Cuentos Del Matador (Tales of the Matador) • Daffodil Caprice • Love Song in the Rain • Midnight Prayer • Nocturne d'Esprit • Rapsodie • Scherzo • Urban Heartbeat.
00193588 ....$10.99

RAGTIME!
Early Intermediate/Intermediate Level
8 original rags from Bill Boyd, Phillip Keveren, Carol Klose, Jennifer Linn, Mona Rejino, Christos Tsitsaros and Jennifer & Mike Watts are featured in this solo piano collection. Includes: Butterfly Rag • Carnival Rag • Jump Around Rag • Nashville Rag • Ragtime Blue • St. Louis Rag • Swingin' Rag • Techno Rag.
00124242 ....$9.99

ROMANTIC INSPIRATIONS
Early Advanced Level
From "Arabesque" to "Nocturne" to "Rapsodie," the inspired pieces in this collection are a perfect choice for students who want to play beautiful, expressive and impressive literature at the recital. Includes: Arabesque • Journey's End • Nocturne • Nocturne d'Esprit • Prelude No. 1 • Rapsodie • Rondo Capriccioso • Valse d'Automne.
00296813.....................................$8.99

SUMMERTIME FUN
Elementary Level
Twelve terrific originals from favorite HLSPL composers, all at the elementary level. Songs: Accidental Wizard • Butterflies and Rainbows • Chill Out! • Down by the Lake • The Enchanted Mermaid • Gone Fishin' • The Merry Merry-Go-Round • Missing You • Pink Lemonade • Rockin' the Boat • Teeter-Totter • Wind Chimes.
00296831 ....$7.99